LIFE INTERRUPTED

ROCHELLE SMITH

Copyright © 2021 by Rochelle Smith

All Rights Reserved. No part of this publication may be reproduced, stored in a retrieval system, or transmitted, in any form or in any means – by electronic, mechanical, photocopying, recording or otherwise – without prior written permission from the author.
ISBN: 978-1-955258-02-9

Scripture references marked KJV are from the KING JAMES VERSION: KING JAMES VERSION, public domain.

Scripture references marked NIV are from the HOLY BIBLE, NEW INTERNATIONAL VERSION®, NIV®. Copyright © 1973, 1978, 1984, 2011 by Biblica, Inc.TM Used by permission of Zondervan. All rights reserved worldwide. www.zondervan.com The "NIV" and "New International Version" are trademarks registered in the United States Patent and Trademark Office by Biblica, Inc.TM
Scriptures marked NLT are taken from the HOLY BIBLE, NEW LIVING TRANSLATION (NLT): Scriptures taken from the HOLY BIBLE, NEW LIVING TRANSLATION, Copyright© 1996, 2004, 2007 by Tyndale House Foundation. Used by permission of Tyndale House Publishers, Inc., Carol Stream, Illinois 60188.

All rights reserved. Used by permission.

Table of Contents

Dedication	5
Preface – Why I chose this title	7
Introduction	9
Life Interruption – I can't breathe	12
Kidney Failure	14
The Eagle	16
Cancer – Not once but twice	22
Cancer – Second time around	26
Determination	27
Restoration	33
God bottles up every tear	35
God's promises to heal us	37
Happiness "During" Life's Interruptions	39
Mark 11:24 – Believe and Receive	41
Victor or Victim	43
Words to live by	45
Choose to believe Him	47
Appendix	48

Dedication

This book is dedicated to my Lord and Savior Jesus Christ. It is because of Him, and Him only that I am able to write this book. He really is Jehovah Rapha and in the darkest of times He has shown His strength, power, and love. I am forever in love with God the father, God the son, and God the Holy Spirit.

Also, to my husband Apostle Price Smith. There are no words to express my gratitude for you standing by my side during these dark times. You bring a new meaning to, "through sickness and health." YOU said it, you meant it, and you have proven it. The enemy challenged us greatly through my health, but I watched your strength, your faith, and your determination to aide me in this vicious journey. Many nights, I woke up to your implementation of the New Testament principle of the laying on of hands partnered with your intercession whilst decreeing the word of God over my life. Thank you so much for being the epitome of an awesome and great man of God.

Preface
Why This Title?

Why did I choose this title? The answer beloved is simple, the Holy Spirit gave it to me. For 10 years, my life was rotationally interrupted by sickness. My daily routine changed drastically. It infuriated me, because at that time I felt like I had no control of my life. My attitude changed, and my mind and my heart needed adjusting in order for me to live my life. I now have a new normal, and this body of work reflects my life for the last 10 years.

Life Interrupted was birthed because God want me to show you the reader, that "in the worst of circumstances, He is still God" and ultimately still in control. Sometimes we become so familiar with our daily routine of life and when it is changed or challenged so does our disposition toward God. Some can't handle change especially if the change is not in their favor. The life I knew prior to illness was no more, and I had to deal with this new life and make the best of it.

Listen, when I say *Life Interrupted*, is comprised around storm, after storm…after storm… after storm! As you sit and read this book, grab your tissue and most importantly grab your praise! One thing to note, this is not a "woe is me" kind of book. This is a "HALLELUJAH!" God did it for ME, and I am sure He can do it for you type of book!

Introduction

Have you ever met anyone that was very familiar with the concept of warfare? How about individuals who experienced extreme disappointment, and discouragement? Are you at all surprised that they managed to overcome everything and walk-in total victory? Well, believe it or not I just described to you the last 10 years of my life. Allow me to take you on a journey. The last 10 years, especially the first eight were full to the brim of extreme warfare. I battled disappointment, discouragement, sickness, and multiples diseases. Yes, I said "multiple diseases". At the same time, while my life was being interrupted with sickness, I was still pastoring a church, counseling other, pursuing my education, and still maintaining my role of wife, and mother. I was determined not to allow kidney failure, cancer, or any other disease for that matter, to stop me from doing what God had called me to do. Let me give you a definition of determination. To be determined is "the act of having firm or fixed intention to achieve a desired result." I was determined that even though my life was interrupted with "sickness and diseases" I was going to live!

With this novel, I want you the reader, to feel and experience with me the nights that I cried out to God, begging for Him to heal me all while the enemy told me that I was dying! Those nights, where I had to battle in prayer and intercession and Holy Spirit literally calmed my fears and rocked me to sleep. Daily, I had to hold fast to the word of God. I want you to see and experience the miraculous healing power of God through this book. Even writing of this book, I am still LIVING with kidney disease. However, I am still determined to live a fulfilled life. How are you living? The dictionary is defining the concept of living by being "full of life or vigor" Even with a disease, God has not allowed me to miss out on anything. I have launched my own coaching business and I am now the author of a book! I am still a wife, mother and Pastor of a wonderful congregation of people. It is true when the scripture states, "what the enemy meant for evil, God has turned it around for my good; for the saving of many lives."

Beloved hold tight to your faith, God keeps us day by day! Job said, "a man born of a woman is of a few days," meaning that we must enjoy the days here on earth that we have. We must not allow sickness, people, things, or anything else to stop us from living each day to the fullest. If someone starts this book, I pray that the beginning captivates their attention, and My heart's desire is to get this book in the hands of every kidney patient and every cancer patient. I'm heralding this message,

"YOU CAN & YOU WILL MAKE IT"

One of my favorite scriptures to use in battle even to this day is, Jeremiah 30:17. The scripture tells us "You said you would restore health unto me, and you would heal me of all of my wounds." I believe and I know that God is a healer! Let me give you a peak into my story.

Life Interruption
(I Can't Breathe)

While at home one day I noticed that it was very difficult for me to walk. Attempting to take even the smallest of steps, I would instantly run out of breath. What was a once 30 second walk would take me ten minutes? I needed the assistance of my husband to do the simplest of chores. After going to the doctor, they informed me that my oxygen levels dropped and that my lungs were bleeding. Wait, what? How? Why? The doctors had no answers. They themselves were baffled. After a four day stay in the hospital, they sent me home with an oxygen tank and a told me to call a specific phone number to schedule my next oxygen delivery. Eventually, I did as I was instructed. When the day arrived, I opened the door, and it was four life size oxygen tanks.

At night the equipment would make the loudest noise and I would lay there and rebuke the enemy. The machinery covered my entire bedroom wall.   My husband would leave for work every morning at 4am. This was our battle scripture. *Mark 11:23 For verily I say unto you that whosoever shall say unto this mountain, be thou removed and be thou cast into the sea and shall not doubt in his heart but shall believe that those things which he saith shall come to pass he shall have whatsoever he saith.*

The equipment was hooked up for two weeks, my husband looked at me one morning in prayer and he said, "in 8 days this equipment is getting out of here!" We both held hands, stood on Mark 11:23 and by faith we believed. My husband said to me directly, "figure out how you want to decorate that wall because those tanks are getting out of here never to return." He also declared that my lungs would bleed no more in Jesus' name! Together, we stood and believed God!

Friend. I want you to know, that on the 8th day, the company came picked up those tanks. My lungs had stopped bleeding, and breathing was back to normal. To this day, my lungs are healthy and whole in Jesus' name! Upon my scheduled doctor's appointment, the doctors were confused. They could not understand how lungs could just stop bleeding without excess medication or surgery. They questioned me asking, "where are your oxygen tanks?" My reply, "God healed me and I don't need them anymore."

Kidney Failure

After being diagnosed as a diabetic, I went one day for my routine appointment. After reviewing all the test results, one of the doctors informed me that I had to get my diabetes under control, and that my creatine number was too high, and this could ultimately lead to kidney failure. I went home and did what was necessary. I changed my diet, started an exercise program and continued with my day-to-day routine. One night specifically, I recall waking up consistently because I kept going to the bathroom. This continued for about a week. I noticed that I was unusually tired all the time and that I had no strength. My strength depleted so badly that my husband started taking me back and forth to go and use the bathroom.

Can you imagine? I could not do anything for myself. Eventually, my husband had to comb my hair, bath me, feed me, etc. I felt worthless as a wife. Everything that needed to be done, he was there to do it without complaints. My body swelled, I experience consistent fever, nausea, heart palpitations. Those were just a few of my symptoms. Finally, my husband said, "You're going to the emergency room." When we arrived at the emergency room and the only thing, I could remember was being probed with all kinds of tubes in me. I could hear them saying "her kidneys are failing" repeatedly. Aside from the kidneys failing, the diabetes was also out of control. My hemoglobin had dropped so low that I really was facing the door of death.

It was at that moment, where the doctors told my husband "She is not going to make it". My husband's response was "Oh yes she is! "She will live and not die." For four days I laid there, not knowing everything that had occurred. I was oblivious to what was going on around me. When I opened my eyes, I didn't see either my husband or any of the doctors. Instead, I saw this white eagle. He stood from ceiling to floor in the corner of my room. His eyes were staring directly at me. Piercing, without motion, or movement. His eyes were direct. They were fixed on me as if staring at the core of my very being! It was in that moment that I heard Holy Spirit say to me, "I am here." I knew at that moment, that I was going to live. A few days later the doctors came and gathered around my bedside as they normally would and said to me these very words, "young lady, you are a miracle!" I recall them shaking my husband's hand saying, "Your faith is what made this possible!" My husband never left my side. He stayed with me all nine nights. He slept on the couch in the room. When the hospital staff brought me breakfast and lunch, they would bring him the same.

The Eagle

What I felt in my hospital room was the presence of the Lord. Prophetically, an eagle represents courage, strength, power and resilience. The eagle also represents new beginnings. The eagle arrived on the scene to make a statement, to give a clarion call and announce that I was about to embark on a new journey. *Deuteronomy 32:11 says, "like an eagle stirs its nest and hovers over its young, that spreads its wings to catch them and carries them aloft."* In this text, Moses was actually talking to the children of Israel. Telling them, that as an eagle stirs her nest and hovers over her young, protecting them from all danger; God was going to carry them out of slavery and continue to protect them as they wandered through the wilderness. That same eagle was sent to protect me.

Friend, if you are experiencing sickness of any kind, remember God is protecting you! He's carrying you! You are protected! There is no need for you to worry.

Isaiah 26:3 says, "I will keep you in perfect peace, if you keep your mind stayed on me." In order to maintain that state of perfect peace during our greatest challenges, we must trust God completely. Trusting God is easier said than done of course, but believe me, when the storms of life rage what is in your soul will come out! You will see how much you actual do in fact trust God. When you attempt to have that perfect peace, you cannot focus on how you feel or what others are saying. Scripture is very clear on how we need to keep our complete attention on God. At one point, I had to speak directly to myself. My exact words were – "Rochelle you will have peace of mind. You do have the mind of Christ. I only think on whatsoever is lovely, whatsoever is pure ect." Sometimes you just got to speak and prophesy over yourself. God said in *Isaiah 43:2, "When you pass through the waters, I will be with you and through the rivers they shall not overwhelm you. When you walk through fire you shall not be burned, and the flame shall not consume you."* Those who trust God are never alone, even during the worst of times. God is with you. In having perfect peace know that there is no stress, no worry, and no second-guessing what God has said.

The term perfect peace is really coined from the word "Shalom, Shalom." In the Hebrew language, repetition infers intensity. It is not just a shalom, it is "shalom, shalom." Perfect peace is God implying, the concept of "double" for your trouble. In Shalom, there is no room for irritability, sadness, or worry! This is because Jehovah Shalom has entered the scene.

As the Prince of Peace, your heart has to literally stop and embrace God. He has the ability to take you to a place that is so serene. Although you are going through, and Hell has broken loose, there can be "Shalom, shalom" Perfect peace can only come from God. Beloved, hold on to God's peace as you continue to fight the good fight of faith! Stand strong and remember that there is hope and peace in God. There is healing for you. Be encouraged and keep fighting!

One thing I found most interesting while engaging with my own warfare, was the battle in my emotions. It is here where you find out what you are made of. Will you continue to trust God and stand on His word? Or will you let disappointment and unbelief take you out?

If you have ever had to battle a chronic disease, you know that there are times when you want to give up. Walk with me through one of the most terrifying days of being a dialysis patient. For those of you that are familiar with a dialysis clinic, you understand that there are about thirty patients in one huge room. Each patient is connected to their own machine. On a particular day, I was not feeling my best. All of a sudden, while connected to my machine, I began to feel lightheaded. The room started spinning and I don't remember a thing after that. The correct term for this is "bottom out". Obviously, my blood pressure dropped so low that they had to throw ice cold water on me and slap me back to life. Yes, I said, "slap me back to life". I woke up to my technician slapping me as if we were in the boxing ring. I cried all day asking God if this was what I had to look forward to for the rest of my life. All I remember was being soaking wet, with a group of nurses standing around me, and one particularly slapping me with all she had. With dialysis, it oftentimes takes a while for the blood pressure to raise to normal levels. During this time, you are weak, lightheaded, and it is hard to comprehend most things going on around you.

When experiencing different trials and tests, you are going to need a support system. I have an amazing support system which is my wonderful husband who has stood by me through every challenge. He has been 1000% in my corner. He certainly brings a new meaning to the vow "in sickness and in health". My children, Lachelle & CJ have been the best through all of this, praying with me every step of the way. Our leadership staff at the church has been so loving and kind, assisting us with anything that is needed. They are truly an amazing group of people.

I would recommend that if you have a love one dealing with a particular disease, try to learn all about that disease so you can assist them with living their best life. One must understand what the body goes through, especially for patients who are connected to a dialysis machine three days a week.

To every dialysis patient: look at your life this way. Instead of dreading your 3 days a week experience, begin to thank God that he is using this procedure right now to help save your life. If it were not for the machines right now, toxins would build up in your system and you could dead by this time tomorrow. God is using dialysis to save you. To this day, I press my way to the dialysis clinic and like you; they have to clean my blood and flush the toxins out of my body too. I go into the clinic with my worship music and my word. I read, I worship and sometimes I sleep. I challenge you to look at your experience in a positive way instead.

It amazes me, that some people think that because you are laughing, talking, and seemingly alright that you don't have any struggles. I've been told on numerous occasions that I did not look like I was a dialysis patient. I attribute that to my heavenly father who said he would "renew my youth like the eagle". He renews, restores, and refreshes my spirit daily! Oh, how I can't live a day without Him! I now get to share this testimony with so many people. You can't look at me and tell I'm on dialysis. I live every day as if it's my last. My mindset is until God give me a kidney; I'm going to enjoy every day! I refuse to feel sorry for myself. I am too busy living!

.

CANCER
NOT ONCE BUT TWICE

My first battle with cancer

I had been diagnosed with thyroid disease. The day before my surgery as I was praying, and I had a vision of the Lord holding my hand. I began to rejoice because the Lord confirmed to me that during this surgery, He would be with me. While they were prepping me for surgery, I began to feel very uneasy, and I became frantic. I knew something was wrong. They ended up giving me a sedative to calm me down. After the surgery I woke up with a trach in my throat. Not knowing what had happened I began to cry. It was then the doctors explained to me what really happened during my procedure.

When they went to take the thyroid out, they found a tumor in the back of my throat and that tumor was indeed cancerous. On top of that, my lungs collapsed twice! Yes, twice. On the table and they had to bring me back, which is why the trach was put in my throat. According to the doctors, I died on the operating table not once, but *twice*.

The trach stayed in for 30 days. During this time, I watched my mother take care of me and my dad who was battling a separate sickness all at the same time. Thank God for mothers! I watched her lay on the floor and intercede for us both. Prayer works!

My children would call me while in the hospital and we came up with this code. I would knock on the phone once if I was ok. Knock twice if I needed them or if something is wrong. I could not talk for an entire week. I had to communicate in other methods. By knocking or writing notes.

When I finally was able to go to my home, they gave me radiation therapy. I had to be away from my children again for ten whole days. All of the above came from a routine thyroidectomy, which is usually an outpatient surgery. It turned into a major two-month issue… but God!

One thing about this battle while in the hospital with the trach in my throat, my grandmother who at the time was at least 80 made her way to the hospital and laid her hands on me. Oh, how that blessed my soul. Granny Mo did not care about elevators and she made it known when she got to the room! (LOL). She was determined to lay hands and pray. I honor those matriarchs that laid the foundation for me in prayer. I have had some great examples in my life.

Friend, I said that to say this, healing from any prognosis is possible! God started my healing process in my heart and in my mind first. Mentally and emotionally, I refused to be sad or fearful. I was (and still am) determined to live a happy life. I refuse to let what I'm dealing with keep me in a box. I made up my mind that I would start my business, write this book, and accomplish whatever my heart desired.

While we are in our storms of life, we must fight! I had to literally fight to come up out of depression, and discouragement. I had to fight to keep my faith and fight to keep my mind focused. Every time a sickness arose, whether it was dialysis or my lungs bleeding, I had to fight. I fought with the Word of God and Faith! When disappointment, fear and anger would try to take over, I would quickly grab the weapon of the word of God and fight. One scripture that ministers to me to this day is Psalms 119:71. It states that, "It was good for me to be afflicted so that I might learn your decrees." While we are our battles, sometimes we can't see what God is doing. In all honesty, that can be frustrating, and it can make you feel forsaken. Praise God that storms don't last always. We serve a God that will not only show you the purpose of the storms, but He will give you reason to thank Him in the storm! I now realize that God was perfecting some things in me, (and he is still perfecting me). At the same time, He was showing me that He honors his word. His word to me during those trials was truly more necessary than the food I ate. Job 23:12 states, "I have not departed from the commands of his lips." Eventually, after every storm, you become skillful at using the word of God. Holy Spirit begins to show you how to decree with power and authority. The storms of life will come indeed, just make sure you know the One who can calm them.

Cancer
The Second Time Around

One day I am visiting my doctor for my routine appointment. At this particular appointment, I asked the nurse to examine a growth I had found on my breast. It was about the size of a walnut that seemed to appear out of nowhere. She agreed to perform a biopsy and would notify me of my results. After three days, the doctor called me and shared with me that the growth was cancerous. I was speechless. My husband broke the silence that was almost deafening with "our God is still God, just like he healed you before He will do it again". Instantly, my faith was charged, and we began to pray. I went through the first assigned surgery successfully. The following week, the doctors called back and informed me that they should perform another surgery to ensure they removed all what was cancerous. After deliberating, I agreed, and the second surgery was a success! I was diagnosed with cancer twice, and currently there is no trace of cancer nowhere in my body. God performed a miracle, and with no chemotherapy!

Determination

When I coach people, I coach them from a place of determination, and I help them focus on what they really want out of life. Healing, for me, started one day as I was lying in a hospital bed listening to the doctors give their negative reports. While they were talking, I would imagine playing ping pong. Yes, ping-pong. My thought process was "you bounce it on me, I bounce it back on you." I refused to receive any negative reports. I was determined to live.

So here is the takeaway from this: Receiving healing is an active concept of faith. We have to actively move towards healing. The first thing that I had to do for my healing, was change my mindset. I had to think on the word of God. In the mind of God, He healed me over 2,000 years ago and I had to mentally jump on that band wagon! I had to really believe that even though all this was happening to me, in the mind of God I am already healed! (Please re-read that sentence). You have to be careful and not allow disappointment to take root in your spirit. It will keep you on a rollercoaster of depression, going up and down, up and down. Disappointment keeps you wondering "Why me?". You are asking questions like; what did I do to deserve it? Is God mad with me? You start reviewing your whole life and contemplating the thought of "maybe I'm being punished. The enemy will sow all kinds of thoughts of doubt and fear when you open the door to him.

You have to block all of the negative thinking because that it is a trick of the enemy. Disappointment and discouragement are major roadblocks to your healing. When discouragement would come, I would command it by the power and authority of Jesus Christ, to go! I had to shake off that disappointment and begin to look at myself as a child of God, no matter what I was going through. I would say things like, "I am the beloved." "I am His and He is mine." "He loves me just like He loves everybody else." So, in order for me to truly receive my healing I had to first be changed in my heart and my mind. Do not look at the situations from a wounded perspective. Look at your situation from a place of victory.

My days are now filled with purpose. During my day, I make sure to engage with my schoolwork, pray for people, minister the word of God by giving godly coaching sessions. I have never been the one to sit around and watch tv and not do anything. I don't have time to be depressed!

When I recognized that discouragement, fear, doubt, depression, were in me, I had to allow God to correct and deliver me. I had to change my mindset concerning, all of those things. I had to cast down imaginations and truly think on the things of God. My focus was found in Philippians 4:8 that said, "Finally brothers and sisters, whatever is true, whatever is noble, whatever is right, whatever is pure, whatever is lovely, whatever is admirable, if anything is excellent or praiseworthy, think about such things." There was constant warfare but once I took ahold of the concepts, there was a major shift and transformation took place in my heart, mind and soul.

Now let's deal with the concept of fear. Fear has tried to grip me in the middle of the night, or when I was at home alone. It would herald out very loud accusations and tried to convince me that what I was believing God for would never happen. Fear must be confronted! You must confront the spirit of fear even if and when you are afraid! Once I confronted fear, the boldness of God came upon me and Holy Spirit took over. Every time I found myself at the hospital, (and there were many) the enemy would whisper "This is it; you are not going home, you are going to die." I would have to rise up and declare, "Not only am I going home, I intend on having a powerful healing and deliverance service, so you just get ready to be cast out." I would say this confident knowing I had all of the authority of Heaven backing me up.

When we operate in fear, God cannot work! You are not operating in faith when fear is present, and you cannot hear from God if there is no faith. The scripture says, in Hebrews 11:6, that "without faith it is impossible to please God." So, there is no way I could stand on the word of God and operate in fear at the same time. Our God is mighty in battle! He's Jehovah Gabor! He is a Mighty Man of War!

To help you understand a little better, I'm going to give you 5 key words to encapsulate the last 10 years of my life.

Believe- For the past 10 years I have stood on **Mark 11:24 "Therefore I tell you whatever you ask in prayer believe that you receive it, and it will be yours."** I have believed through doctor reports, through pain and crying tears that seemed to be never ending. I believed that God was going to spare my life and make everything well. I decreed and declared this scripture daily.

Tears- I have probably cried an entire ocean full of tears within the last decade. I wanted the sickness to cease! Concerning my health, it was always something wrong. I wanted to go back to what I called my "normal life." I spent much time crying out to God and praying. David declared in **(Psalms 56:8) You keep track of all my sorrows. You have collected all my tears in your bottle. You have recorded each one in your book.** Can you imagine God caring so much about us, that He keeps track of our tears! So many times, in the spirit, I would literally see bottles lined up and I knew what God saying to me. He would let me know by saying, "I have your tears and I have them in bottles, and I am going to pour those tears out upon you." Because those tears eventually will become tears of joy. Glory to God, I bless Him for those moments.

Determined- This was and still is a daily mindset! I had to be determined to see victory while taking medication, while sitting at dialysis for three hours, three days a week. My mindset was focused on the word of God. My heart was changed from the hopeless state of "Why me", to "Thank God that even in this; He is still Jehovah Rapha, my healer!" In every situation, as children of God must see Him and choose victory. Otherwise, we will be defeated, and God has not designed any defeat for his children. Remember nothing can stop a determined person – NOTHING!

Growth- All of these interruptions in my life has produced an abundance of Growth. As Betty Wright said, "No pain, no gain!"

Restoration

Whatever you have lost, whether it's health, finances, Joy, etc., our loving Father will restore it.

The enemy will always try to attack our joy. Remember the joy of the Lord is our strength (Nehemiah 8:10). Our adversary loves when we have pity parties because of our circumstances. Your joy is key. How do we receive joy? By spending time with the Lord. As we spend time with God, we have the awesome opportunity to experience the purest of love, peace and joy. Webster's definition of joy is, "a feeling of great pleasure and happiness." Who does not want joy? I refuse to spend time in pity, despair or discouragement. I am not saying we will not be attacked in this area. What I am saying is the minute you recognize these spirits attacking you, choose to fight back immediately. How do we fight back? With the word of God, spending time in prayer and in worship. Do not allow disappointment or any other spirit that is not of God get comfortable in your life.

On the days that you think you cannot make it; those are the days that you have to fight the hardest. You must stand on the word of God. There is the parable of the fig tree which is found in Luke 13:6-9. This shows us the faith that is needed to conquer every day. Jesus cursed that tree and that tree never bore fruit again. We have the power and the authority to curse sickness, so that it will never bear fruit in our lives again.

God Bottles Up Our Tears

In Psalm 56:8, God reminds us that He is concerned with every aspect of our lives intimately. His compassion towards us is truly amazing. He catches every tear that we shed. It does not matter how trivial the situation is, God cares. God is there to wipe away every tear. With this Psalms, David expressed grief over his situation, which was very dangerous. Saul wanted his own son to be King of Israel and was hunting David down, in order to murder him. David was grieved, he was fearful, and he was unsure about his future. Apparently, in this, David began to cry a river of tears. This scripture came out of his spirit. David declared, "you keep track of all of my sorrows…"

When interruptions come in life, whether it be sickness, financial hardship, concerns about the future or general situations that are beyond our control, it is ok to allow the tears flow. When you read this Psalms 56, you can see how passionate David was as he was pouring out his heart to God. It is awesome to know that every one of our sorrows and every one of our pains, He has recorded each one in a book. How awesome is it to know that every time we shed tears, God takes notice of it? According to the text, David drew comfort in knowing that no matter what he was going through, God had great compassion towards him. David had to trust God with his life and with his future and we have to do the same.

The fact that God keeps my tears in a bottle proves that he is with me all the time and that he cares for me more than I could ever care for myself. Jehovah Shammah, according to Ezekiel 48:35 indicates to me that God is present and is always there. When your life is interrupted, you have to trust God. We have to trust what is said in Jeremiah 29:11, where God declares "I know the plan that I have for you and those are those plans are good…"

He is in the midst of our pain, our healing, and our triumph! Every tear that I shed, God manages to contain them and put them away. Sorrow, sickness, and pain will not last always. Even in the midst of them God will allow joy to come, if we receive it. Having joy is a choice. It's up to us to choose.

God Promises to Heal Us

God's original intention was for us to be in good health. When the world was first created, the Bible records that, "God saw everything that He had made, and indeed it was good." (Genesis 3) Disease and death only entered into the world after Adam and Eve disobeyed the Lord and allowed satanic forces to gain a foothold on humankind. Living a life in complete healing is the will of God for you. Why? Because He loves you. He is Jehovah Jireh, and He provides our every need. For those who suffer with chronic illness, being healed is a need. God will not withhold healing from His children.

Jesus is the Great Physician. As I read in Matthew 4:23, I admire how willing Jesus was to heal every disease! This is what the scripture declares, "He healed all kinds of sickness". When you look at the life of Jesus, you will see He did not tolerate sickness. Today is still the same, sickness cannot stand in the presence of God. Be healed today. Sickness is not in the character of God. God is sovereign and God wants the best for His children.

Picture this: You're standing in sinking sand. As hard as you try to climb out, you're sinking deeper and deeper. You fight against it. As the sand rises to your neck and you're about to go under, you spot someone standing in all white, ready to pull you out. You cry. The moment where you thought "this is it", you the decide to grab onto Him, and you are pulled to safety. You finally receive your help! That's how God comes on the scene. He shows up and he delivers!

If anybody is familiar with the presence of God, He comes and literally melts your heart away. The presence of God is so unlike anything else. When He steps into the room, I believe that you are, (or should be) at full attention. The only way that we can miss the presence of God is if we don't know His presence. If we are familiar with His presence, when He comes into the room, there is such a hush. There is such a stillness, especially when you're going through affliction. There is literally a cloud that hovers over your atmosphere. He is there to let you know that everything is well.

Here are a few of my scriptures that I decreed and declared daily. Allow these to deliver you: 3 John 12, Habakkuk 9:37, Luke 16:19, Hebrews 13:8, Isaiah 50:3-5, and Psalm 103:2-3.

Happiness "During" Life's Interruptions

How can this be? You mean to tell me that I can be happy during the most crucial times of my life?! You may say, "You can't possibly understand what I'm facing. I'll be happy when this is over." Trust me, I hear you. That is the response from most people facing Life's Interruptions. What if I told you that in spite of your problems, issues, circumstances, you can still be happy. You see, happiness is a choice. You can either choose to be happy or you can choose to be sad. As I said in the previous chapter, you are either a victor or a victim. You choose. I choose to be happy. I choose to declare Psalms 118:24 that says, "this is a day that the Lord has made, I will rejoice and be glad in it." Please note that the scriptures declare "I _**will**_ rejoice and be glad", it is a choice on your part. We have the opportunity to choose every day if we are going to be happy, sad, depressed or joyful. It ultimately is up to us.

God has several scriptures on being happy! I pray that as you read these scriptures that the spirit of gladness overtakes you and that you don't see your problems as huge obstacles, but you see God as the great problem solver. Isn't God awesome?

Psalms 34:8
Oh, taste and see that the Lord is good. Happy is the man who trusts in him!

Proverbs 16:20.
He who heeds the word wisely will find good, and whoever trusts in the Lord, happy is he.

Psalm 144:15
Happy are the people whose God is the Lord

Philippians 4:4
Rejoice in the Lord always. Again, I say rejoice.

Psalms 37:4
Delight yourself also in the Lord, and he shall give you the desires of your heart.

God wants us happy. Do not let a problem, person or thing because you live one more day without true happiness.

Mark 11:24
Believe and Receive

Battling through unbelief

Scripture tells us in Mark 2:3 that we are to, "believe all things are possible." Of course, the enemy will cause you to think on your circumstances until finally you are in a state of unbelief. Overthinking the negative things will cause unbelief and discouragement. You control your thoughts. You can determine what you will think about. Choose to think on the word of God.

Another way to combat unbelief, is to remember what God has already brought you through. Think about those moments where, you knew, it was nobody but God that came in and rescued you. If God brought me out of that then certainly, He could bring me out of this! Think about things that are of a good report.

Concerning the company, you keep. Think about them. Are they speaking death or life? Are they more focused on the ailment and or the promise? Are they encouraging you or pacifying you? Think about Job. His wife told him to curse God and die. Can you imagine how Job felt as his wife uttered those words? It is imperative that the company you keep have your merit of faith or a much greater capacity of faith.

Victor or Victim

When storms of life rage, we must be careful not to take on the victim mentality. The enemy's plan is to get you stuck in a rut. Once you are stuck, it takes Holy Spirit to deliver you out of it. For me, constant doctor visits, having pain throughout the day and night, it seemed that nothing was going as expected. When you constantly dwell on the negative consistently you are subconsciously developing a "victim mentality".

How do you press beyond this? I'm glad you asked. God made us to have dominion, to conquer, and to be victorious. Anything that is opposite of that you must believe you are "more than a conqueror". Conclude within yourself that, "This will not take me down, nor will it take me out." There are many days encourage me in the Lord. It is all about what you are feeding your spirit. During the times of pain what do you find yourself saying? Are you speaking the word of God in faith? Or are you allowing a few other choice words to come out of your mouth.

There is a big difference between being a victor and a victim.

Here are a few example phrases:

Victim	Victor
The whole world is against me.	I will conquer the world.
This challenge is so big; I can't move forward.	Sees ways to defeat this challenge and says, "I will not accept defeat."
I am a failure. I can't do anything right.	I take personal responsibility for where I am in life and where I am going.
Depends on others to help them succeed.	Use what I have to succeed, and I depend on God daily.
Nothing ever goes my way.	I am content with what I have. I look forward to building on it.
Always sees closed doors.	Always sees open doors
Critical and Judgmental of others.	Always passionate about other successes
Manipulative: uses people for what they can get.	Inspirational; provokes others to flourish.

CHOOSE to Believe Him!

` I truly believe the word of God, it declares in Hebrews 11:6, that "without faith it is impossible to please God". If we don't believe God, how will we expect Him to do anything for us? God knows when we don't believe Him and knows when we are simply going through the motions. If you don't believe Him, there is no way you could receive his divine healing power. The later part of Hebrews 11:6 reads "anyone who comes to me, must believe that He is and that he is a rewarder of them who diligently seek him". You have to believe that God is THE healer! You must believe that over 2,000 years ago, he made it possible for you to be healed. Ephesians 3:20-21 declares, "God is able to do exceedingly and abundantly above ALL that we can ask or think. But guess what? That works according to the power that is in you".

My prayer is for everyone that reads this book even though your life may have been interrupted, God has given us a plan to deal with those interruptions and that is his word. As you learn Him through the word, you will find that dealing with life's interruptions become easier with God's help. Your interruption might not be sickness, it might be constant financial hardship, or family feuds. Whatever your interruptions are, God will see you through every one of them.

Words to Live By

Here are a couple of scriptures that I chose to live by, and I encourage you to use in your storms.

Hebrew 11:6

"Without faith it is impossible to please God."

Isaiah 40:31

"They that wait upon the Lord shall renew this strength. They shall mount up with wings like an eagle, and they shall run and not be weary. They shall walk and not faint."

Mark 11:24

"Therefore, I tell you whatever you ask for in prayer believe that you have already received it, and it will be yours."

Appendix:

Below are some scriptures that you can use to encourage yourself while waiting for healing. Meditate on these scriptures.

<u>Healing & Love Scriptures:</u>

1 Corinthians 13:1-8

If I speak in the tongues of men or of angels, but do not have love, I am only a resounding gong or a clanging cymbal. If I have the gift of prophecy and can fathom all mysteries and all knowledge, and if I have a faith that can move mountains, but do not have love, I am nothing. If I give all I possess to the poor and give over my body to hardship that I may boast, but do not have love, I gain nothing.

Love is patient, love is kind. It does not envy, it does not boast, it is not proud. It does not dishonor others, it is not self-seeking, it is not easily angered, it keeps no record of wrongs. Love does not delight in evil but rejoices with the truth. It always protects, always trusts, always hopes, always perseveres.

Love never fails. But where there are prophecies, they will cease; where there are tongues, they will be stilled; where there is knowledge, it will pass away.

Romans 5:8

But God demonstrates his own love for us in this: While we were still sinners, Christ died for us.

James 5:14-15

Is anyone among you sick? Let them call the elders of the church to pray over them and anoint them with oil in the name of the Lord. And the prayer offered in faith will make the sick person well; the Lord will raise them up. If they have sinned, they will be forgiven.

Exodus 23:25

Worship the Lord your God, and his blessing will be on your food and water. I will take away sickness from among you

Psalm 63:3

Because your love is better than life, my lips will glorify you.

Isaiah 53:4-5

Surely, he took up our pain
and bore our suffering,
yet we considered him punished by God,
stricken by him, and afflicted.
But he was pierced for our transgressions,
he was crushed for our iniquities;
the punishment that brought us peace was on him,
and by his wounds we are healed

Jeremiah 30:17

But I will restore you to health
and heal your wounds,'
declares the Lord,
'because you are called an outcast,
Zion for whom no one cares.'

Hebrews 13:8

Jesus Christ is the same yesterday and today and forever.

Isaiah 50:3-5

I clothe the heavens with darkness
and make sackcloth its covering."

The Sovereign Lord has given me a well-instructed tongue,
to know the word that sustains the weary.
He wakens me morning by morning,
wakens my ear to listen like one being instructed.
The Sovereign Lord has opened my ears;
I have not been rebellious,
I have not turned away.

Psalm 103:2-3

Praise the Lord, my soul,
and forget not all his benefits—
who forgives all your sins
and heals all your diseases,

Proverbs 4:20:22

My son, pay attention to what I say, turn your ear to my words. Do not let them out of your sight. Keep them within your heart for they are life to those who find them and health to one's whole body.

Smith & Smith Coaching

(Coaching of the Highest Quality)

Top ten reasons to hire a coach:

- You will reduce the number of problems you have
- You will be more effective and influential with others
- You will come out of your comfort zone
- You will accomplish goals, tasks and projects more quickly
- You will be held accountable
- You will be a lot happier, with a happiness that will lasts.

Coaching Experience:

- Trauma, Anxiety and fear of failure
- Relationships
- Spiritual Coaching
  (Getting Closer to God)
- Health/Wellness (Living with chronic disease)

Call now for a free Discovery Session
(773) 567-4333

www.ingramcontent.com/pod-product-compliance
Lightning Source LLC
Chambersburg PA
CBHW041526090426
42736CB00035B/25